SCHIRMER'S LIBRARY OF MUSICAL CLASSICS

Vol. 2138

55 PIANO PRELUDES
By 8 Composers

Albéniz, Beethoven, Chopin, Debussy, Mendelssohn, Rachmaninoff, Ravel, Scriabin

ISBN 978-1-5400-2606-4

G. SCHIRMER, Inc.

DISTRIBUTED BY

7777 W. BLUEMOUND RD. P.O. BOX 13819 MILWAUKEE, WI 53213

www.schirmer.com
www.halleonard.com

CONTENTS

Preludio
from *Cantos de España*

Isaac Albéniz
Op. 232, No. 1

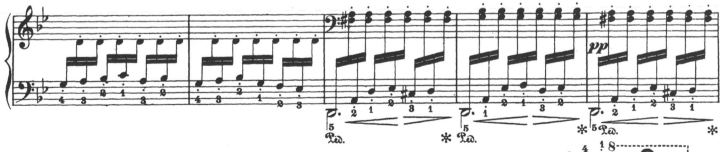

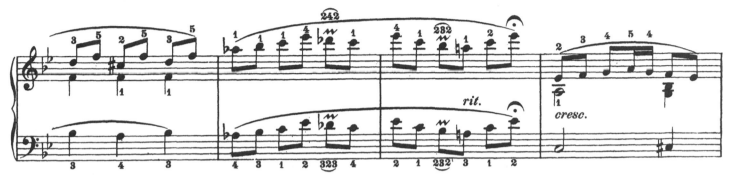

8

Preludio
from *España*

Isaac Albéniz
Op. 165

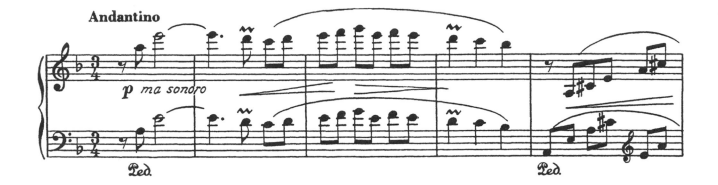

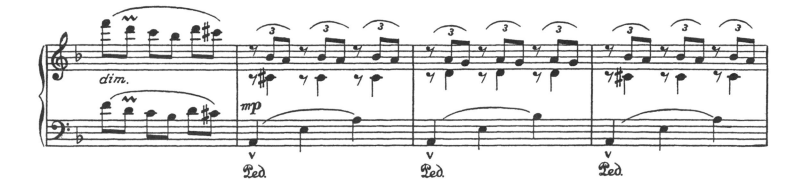

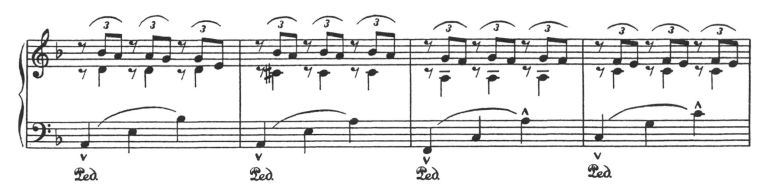

Andante

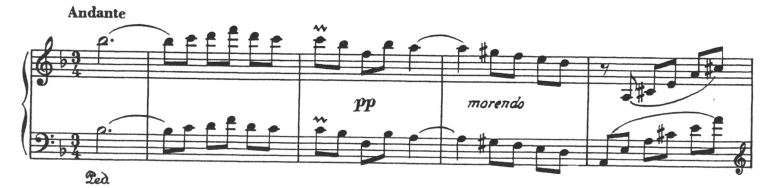

à J.C. Kessler

Prelude
in A minor

Frédéric Chopin
Op. 28, No. 2

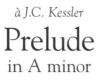

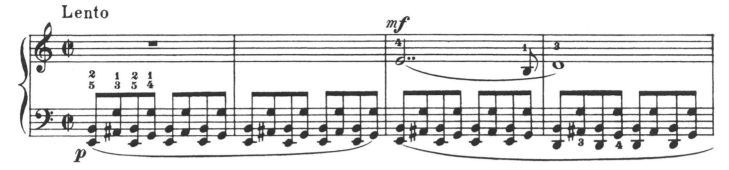

à J.C. Kessler

Prelude
in E minor

Frédéric Chopin
Op. 28, No. 4

à J.C. Kessler

Prelude
in B minor

Frédéric Chopin
Op. 28, No. 6

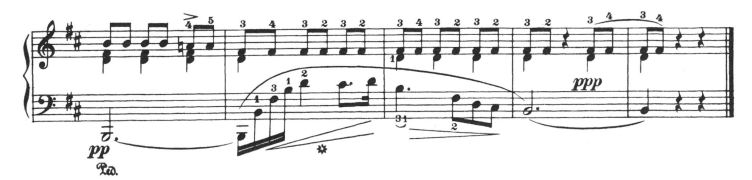

à J.C. Kessler

Prelude
in A Major

Frédéric Chopin
Op. 28, No. 7

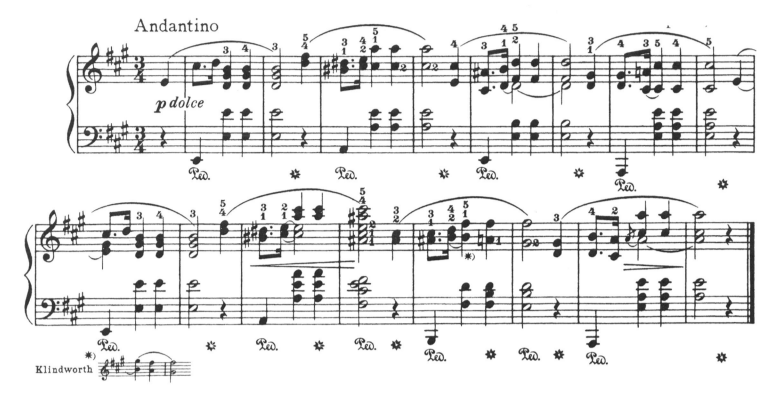

à J.C. Kessler

Prelude
in B-flat Major

Frédéric Chopin
Op. 28, No. 21

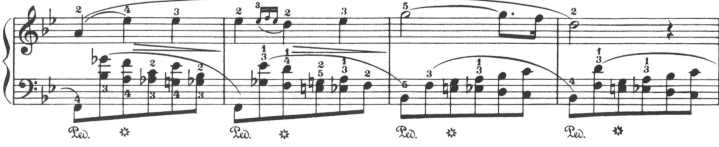

à J.C. Kessler

Prelude
in E Major

Frédéric Chopin
Op. 28, No. 9

*) Scholz:

à J.C. Kessler

Prelude
in F-sharp Major

Frédéric Chopin
Op. 28, No. 13

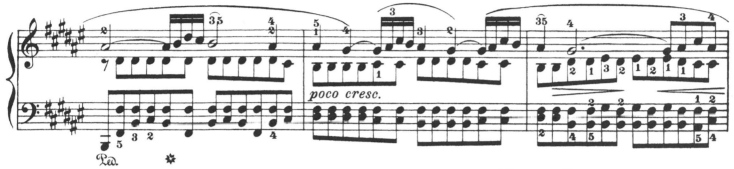

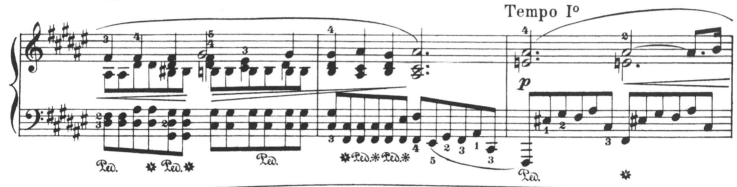

à J.C. Kessler

Prelude
in E-flat minor

Frédéric Chopin
Op. 28, No. 14

Allegro

à J.C. Kessler

Prelude
in D-flat Major

Frédéric Chopin
Op. 28, No. 15

Sostenuto

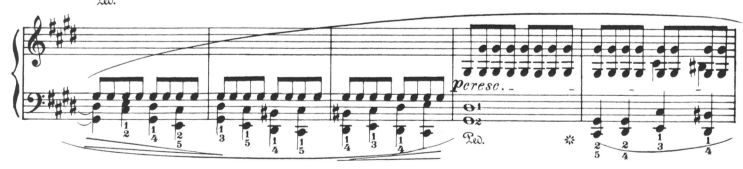

à J.C. Kessler

Prelude
in A-flat Major

Frédéric Chopin
Op. 28, No. 17

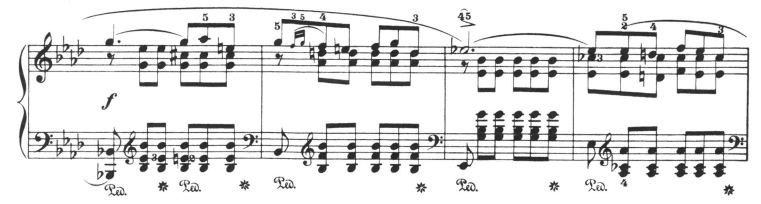

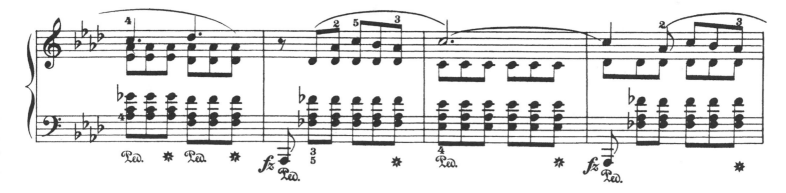

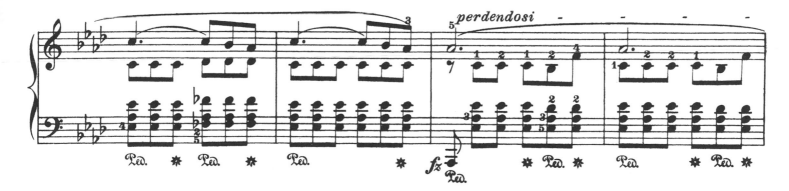

à J.C. Kessler

Prelude
in G minor

Frédéric Chopin
Op. 28, No. 22

Molto agitato

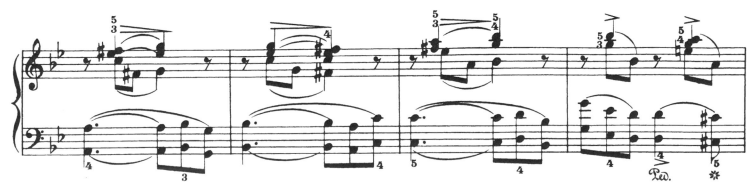
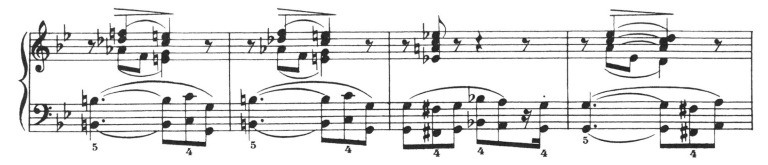

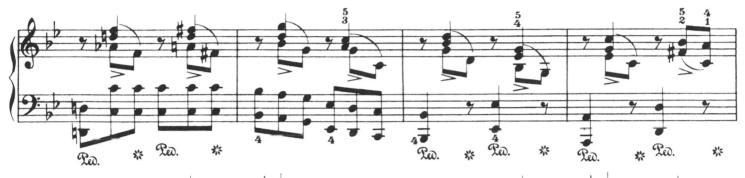

à Mademoiselle la Princessé Élisabeth Czernicheff

Prelude
in C-sharp minor

Frédéric Chopin
Op. 45

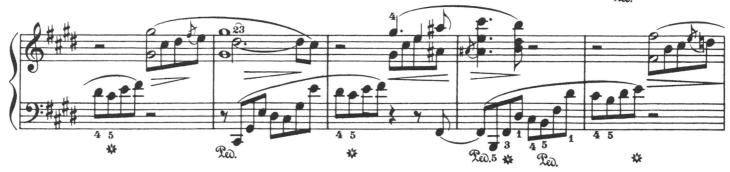

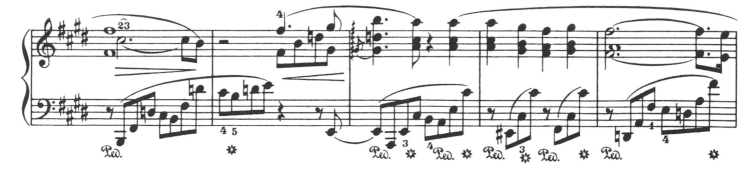

Two Preludes
Through all 12 Major Keys

Ludwig von Beethoven
Op. 39

1

2

42

Danseuses de Delphes

from *Préludes*, Book I

Claude Debussy

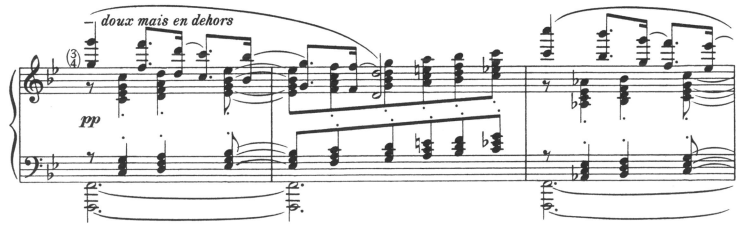

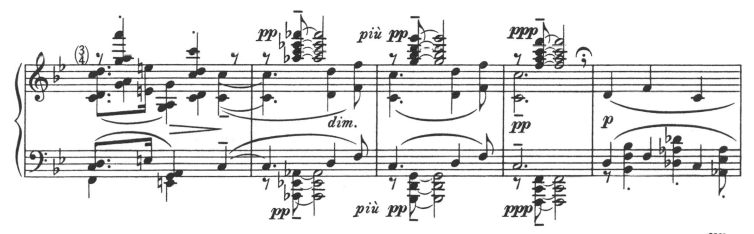

(...Danseuses de Delphes)

Voiles
from *Préludes*, Book I

Claude Debussy

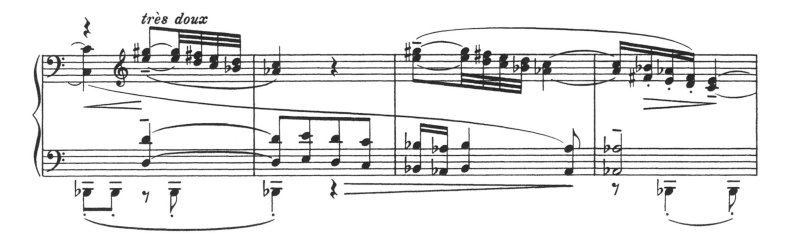

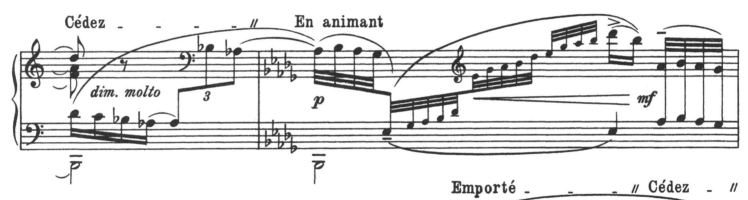

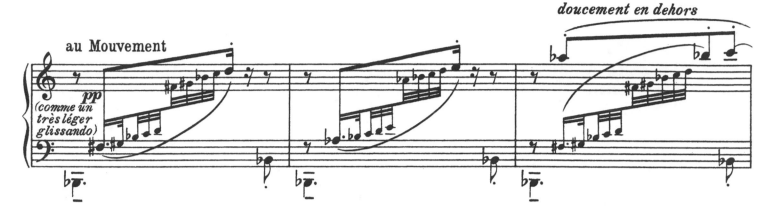

(...Voiles)

"Les sons et les parfums tournent dans l'air du soir"

from *Préludes*, Book I

Claude Debussy

a tempo

pp   pp   p

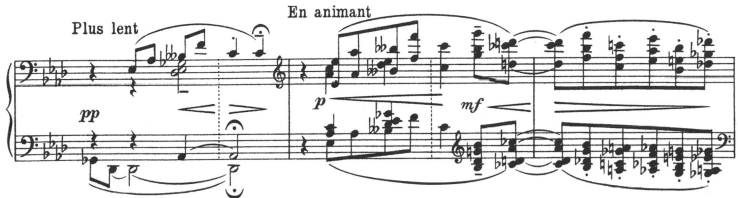

Plus lent   En animant

pp   p   mf

Cédez _ _ _ _ "   Serrez _ _ _ " Rubato

Rubato

pp   mf   p   p

Serrez _ _ _ "

p

la basse un peu appuyée et soutenue

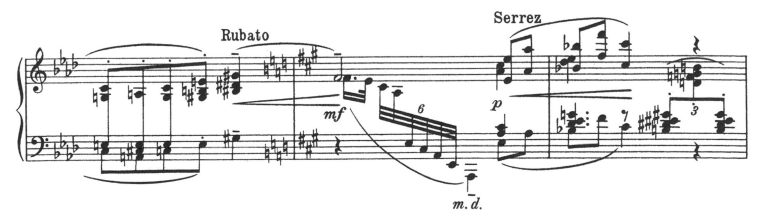

Rubato   Serrez

mf   p

m. d.

(..."Les sons et les parfums tournent dans l'air du soir")

Charles Baudelaire

Des pas sur la neige

from *Préludes*, Book I

Claude Debussy

*Ce rythme doit avoir la valeur sonore
d'un fond de paysage triste et glacé.*

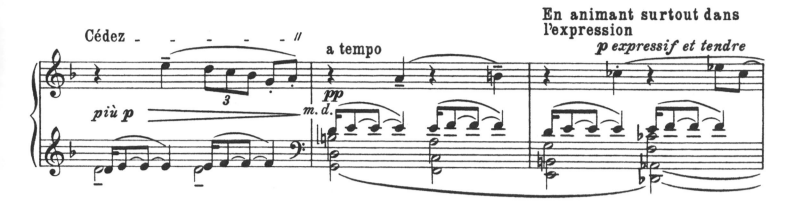

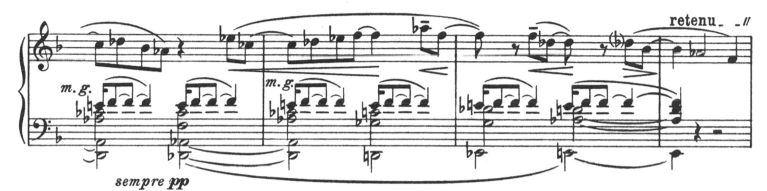

(...Des pas sur la neige)

La fille aux cheveux de lin

from *Préludes*, Book I

Claude Debussy

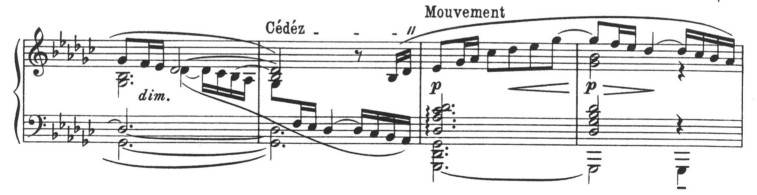

Cédéz _ _ // Mouvement (sans lourdeur)

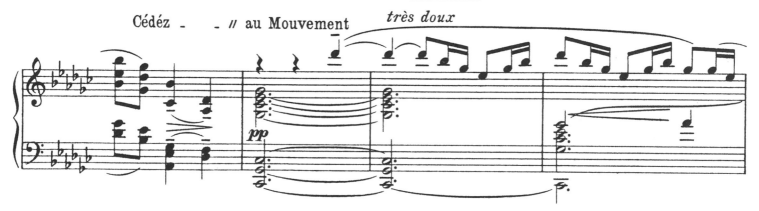

Cédéz _ _ // au Mouvement

très doux

Murmuré et en retenant peu à peu

(...La fille aux cheveux de lin)

La sérénade interrompue

from *Préludes*, Book I

Claude Debussy

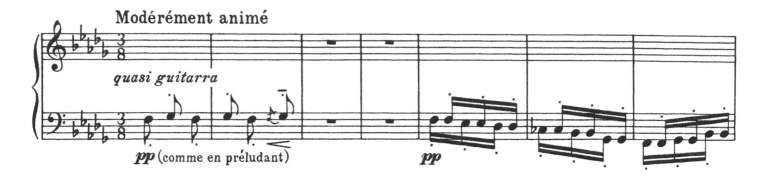

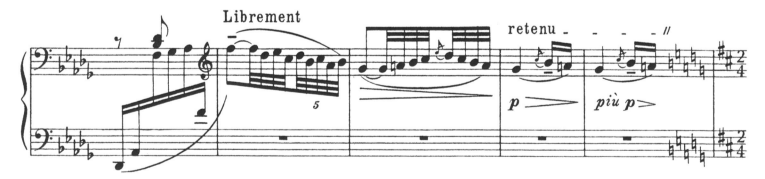

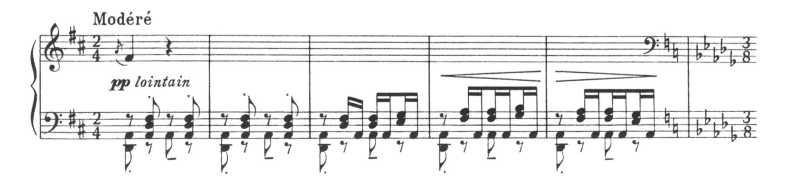

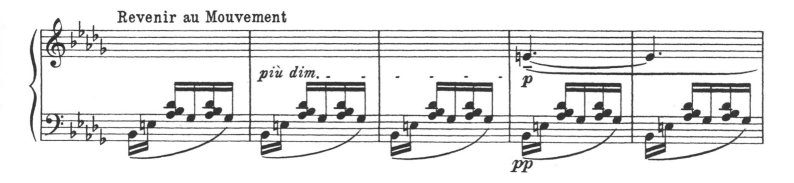

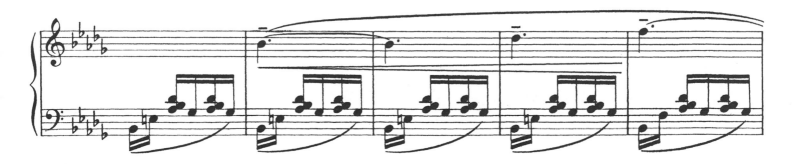

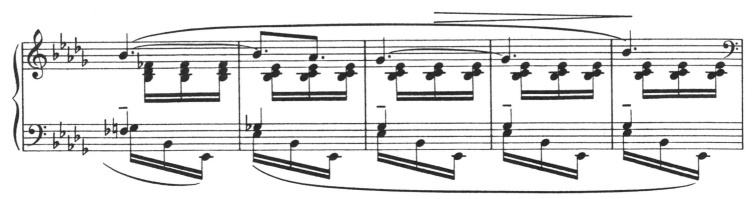

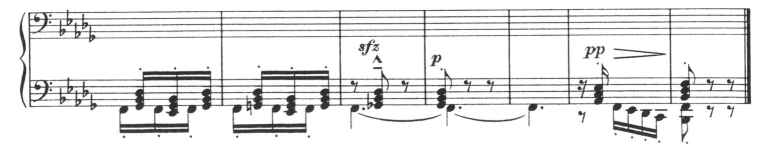

(...La sérénade interrompue)

La Cathédrale engloutie

from *Préludes*, Book I

Claude Debussy

Profondément calme (Dans une brume doucement sonore)

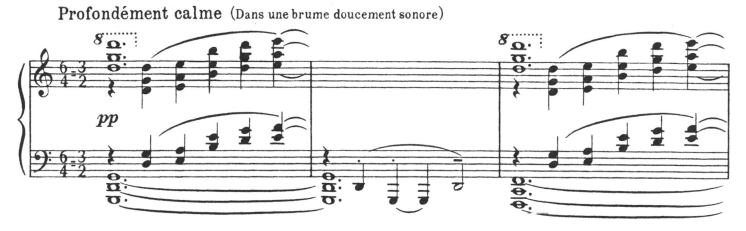

*) Doux et fluide

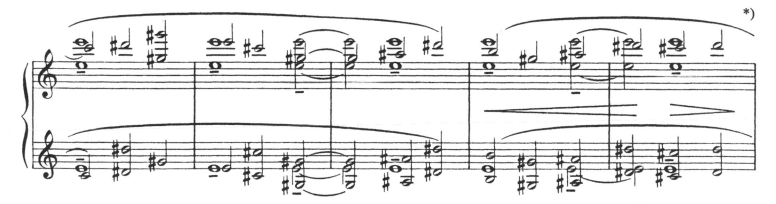

*)

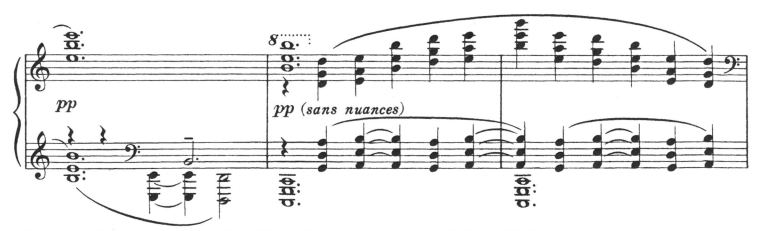

*) Debussy, in his piano-roll recording (Welte-Mignon), played measures 7–12 and 22–83 in double speed.

Peu à peu sortant de la brume

sempre pp

p marqué pp

p marqué pp

p

marqué

Augmentez progressivement (Sans presser)

f

più f

Sonore sans dureté

sff

ff

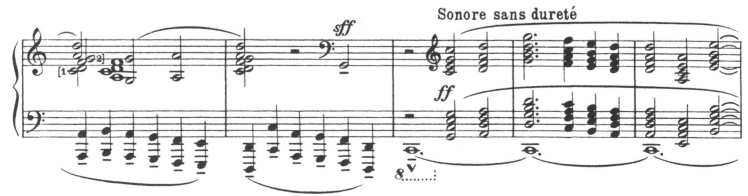

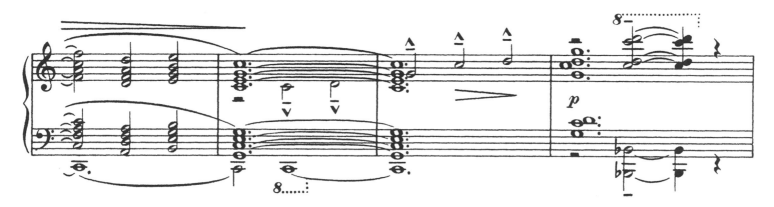

Un peu moins lent (Dans une expression allant grandissant)

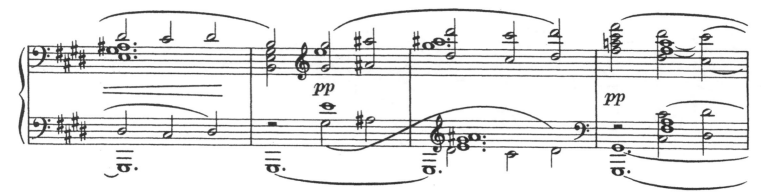

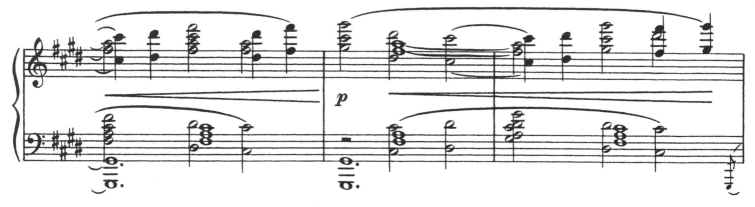

au Mouvement

(...La Cathédrale engloutie)

La danse de Puck
from *Préludes*, Book I

Claude Debussy

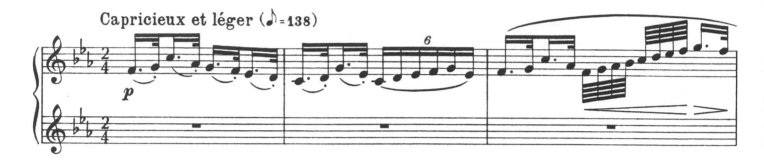

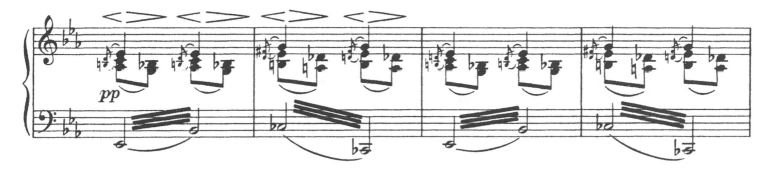

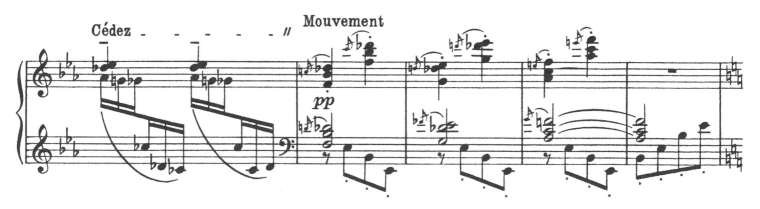

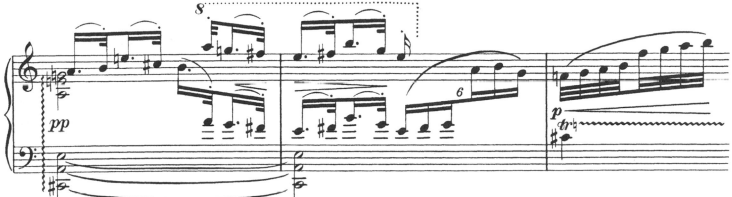

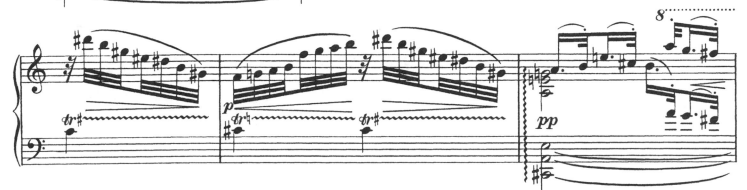

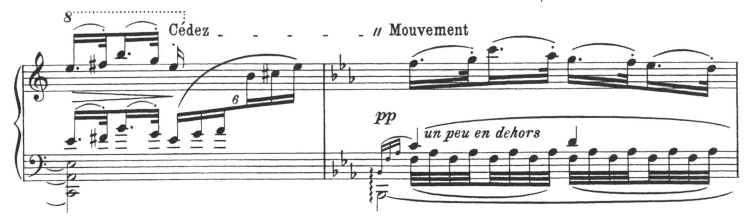

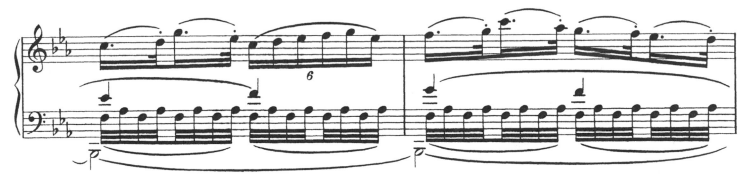

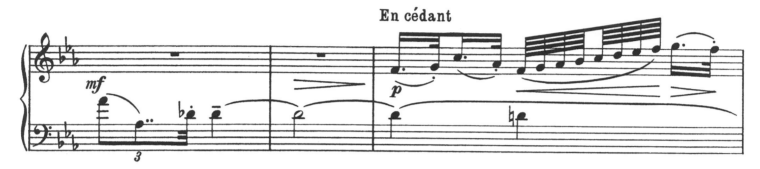

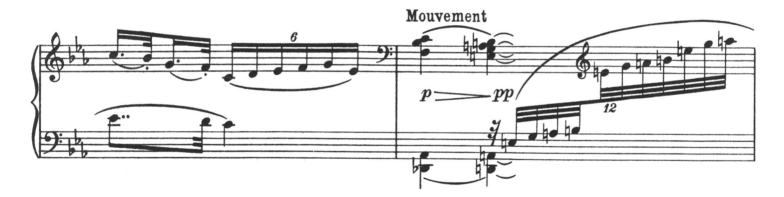

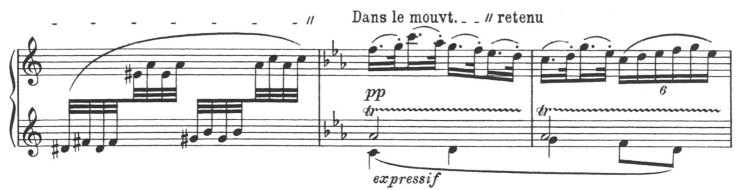

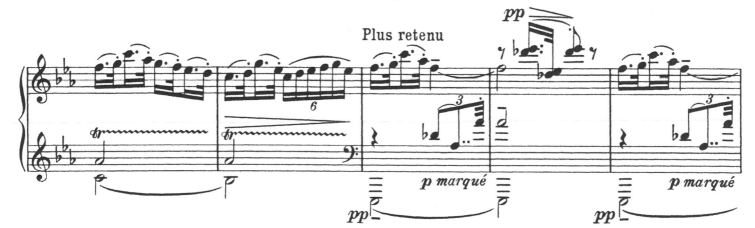

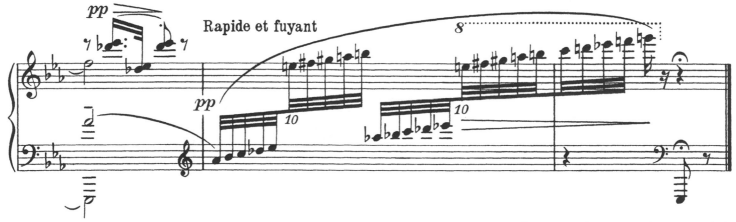

(...La danse de Puck)

Minstrels

from *Préludes*, Book II

Claude Debussy

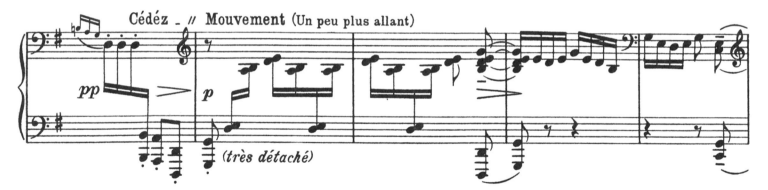

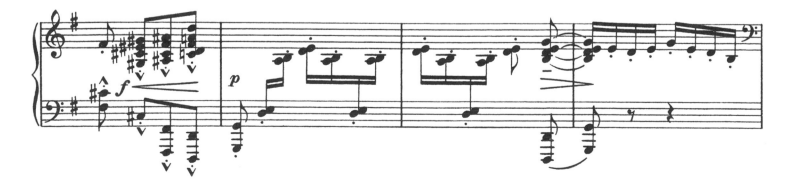

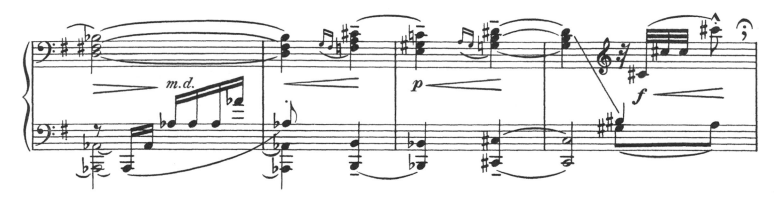

(...Minstrels)

La Puerta del vino

from *Préludes*, Book II

Claude Debussy

Mouvement de Habanera
avec de brusques oppositions d'extrême
violence et de passionnée douceur

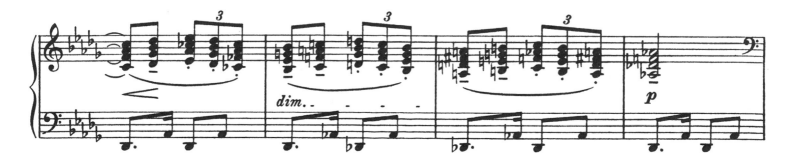

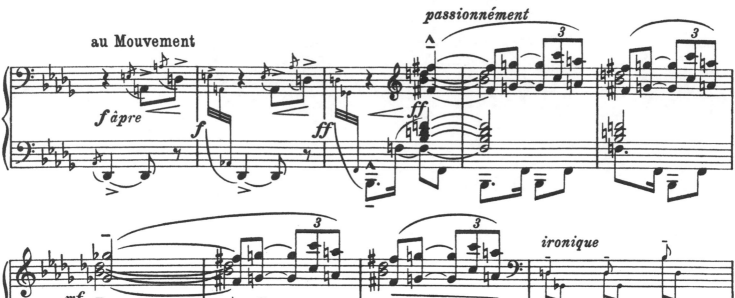

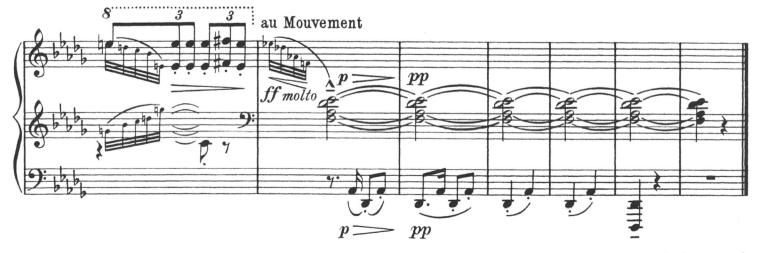

(...La Puerta del vino)

Bruyéres
from *Préludes*, Book II

Claude Debussy

(...Bruyères)

"General Lavine" – *excentric* –

from *Préludes*, Book II

Claude Debussy

Dans le style et le Mouvement d'un Cake-Walk

Spirituel et discret

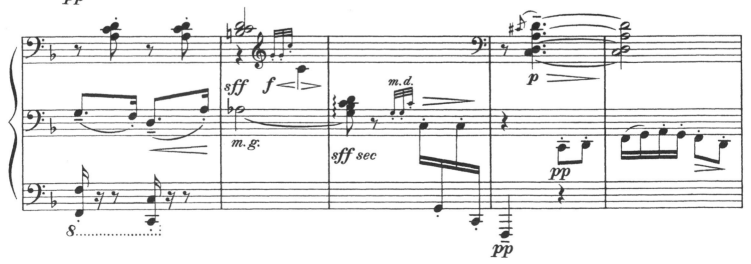

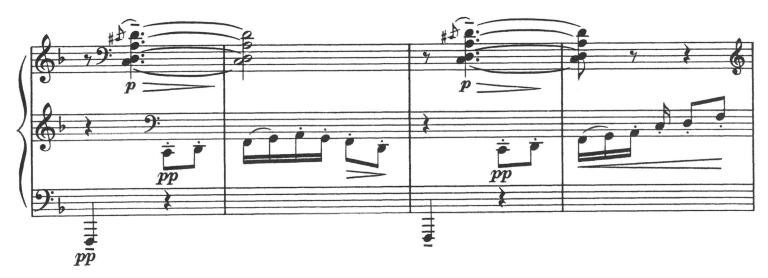

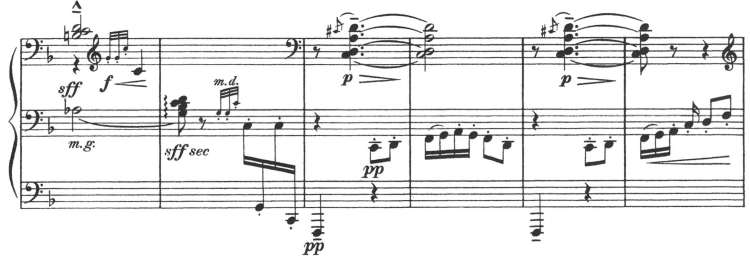

…"General Lavine" – *excentric* –)

Feuilles mortes

from *Préludes*, Book II

Claude Debussy

Lent et mélancolique

doucement soutenu et très expressif

Un peu plus allant et plus gravement expressif

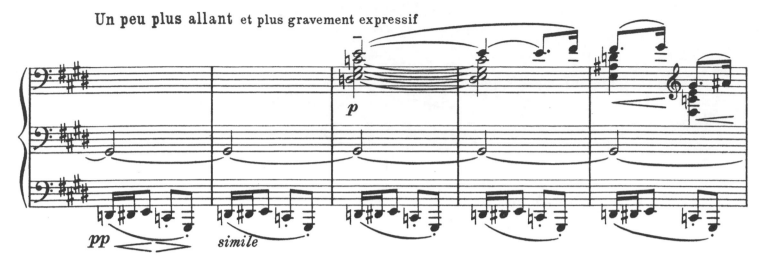

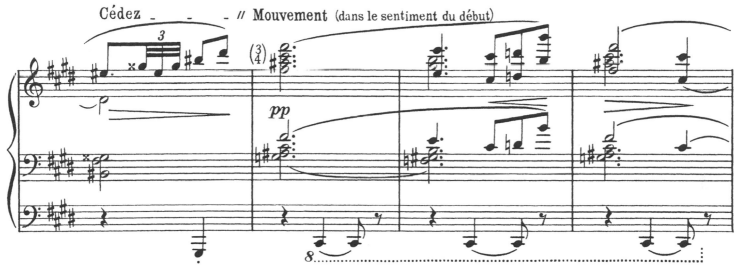

(...Feuilles mortes)

La terrasse des audiences du clair de lune

from *Préludes*, Book II

Claude Debussy

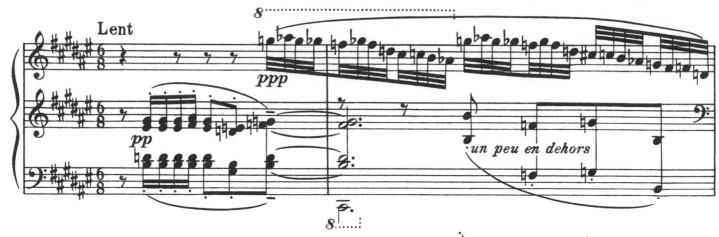

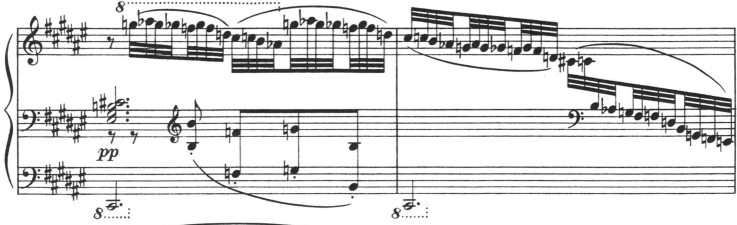

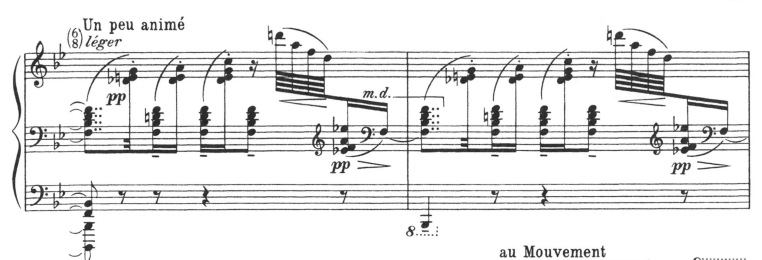

Cédez _ //

Mouvement du début

En animant

Mouvement

(...La terrasse des audiences du clair de lune)

Hommage à S. Pickwick Esq. P.P.M.P.C.

from *Préludes*, Book II

Claude Debussy

Animez peu à peu

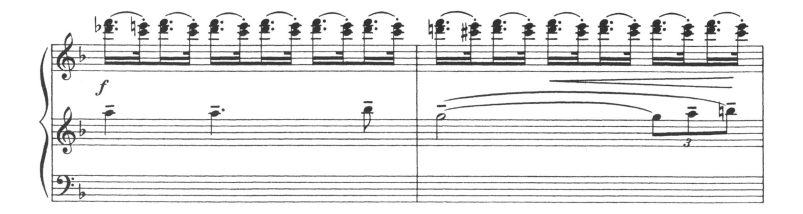

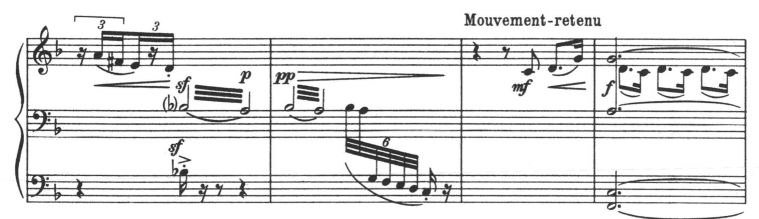

(...Hommage à S. Pickwick Esq. P.P.M.P.C.)

Canope

from *Préludes*, Book II

Claude Debussy

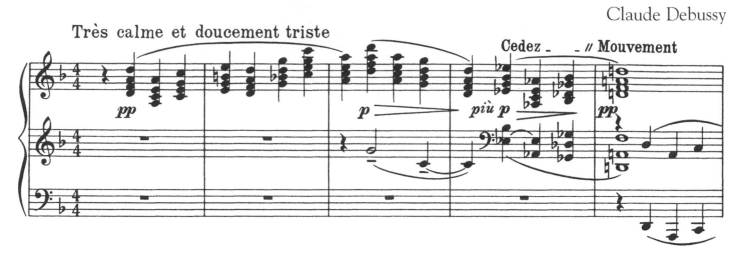

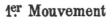

(...Canope)

Prelude
in E minor

Edited and fingered by
Louis Oesterle

Felix Mendelssohn
WoO 13

Prelude
in C-sharp minor

Edited and fingered by
Louis Oesterle

Sergei Rachmaninoff
Op. 3, No. 2

Agitato

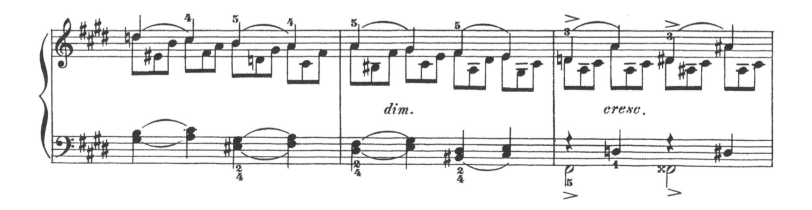

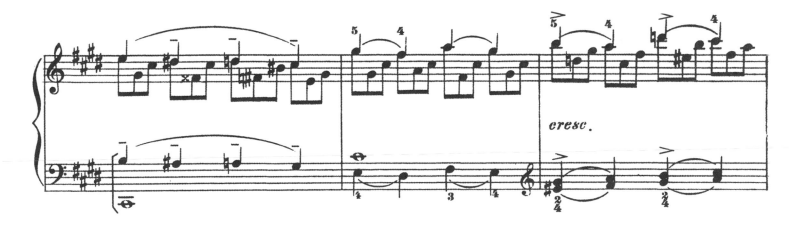

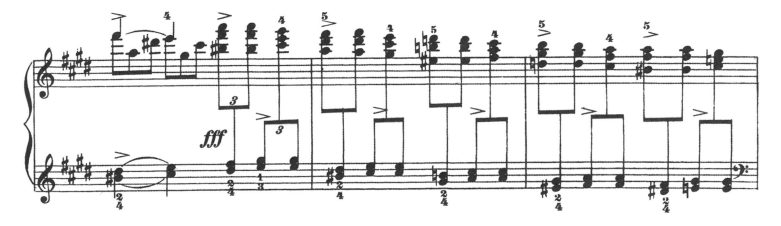

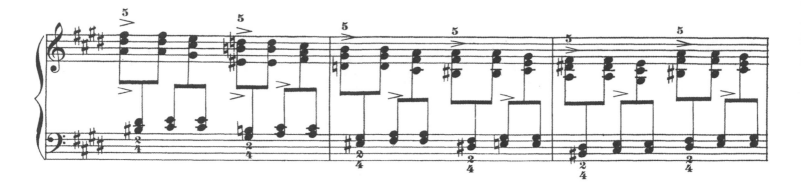

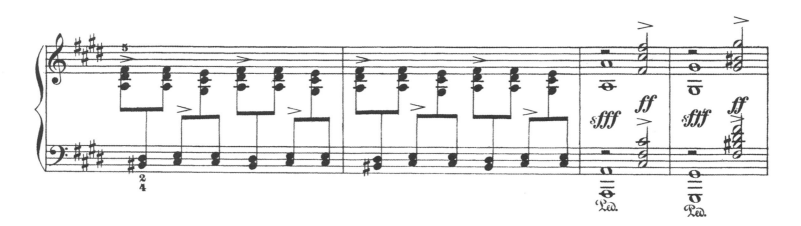

Tempo I

Prelude
in F-sharp minor

Sergei Rachmaninoff
Op. 23, No. 1

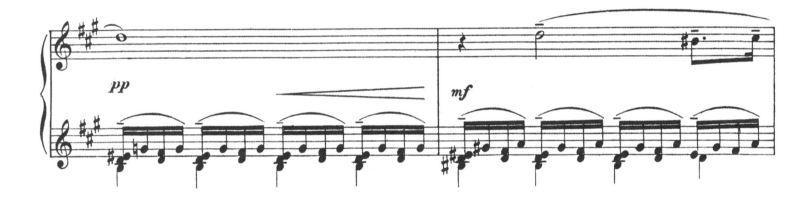

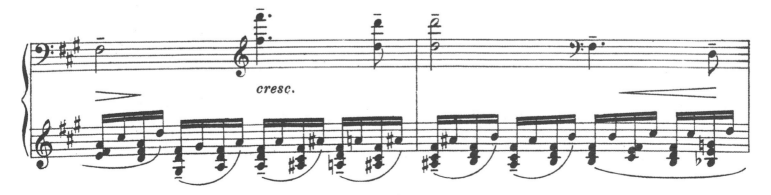

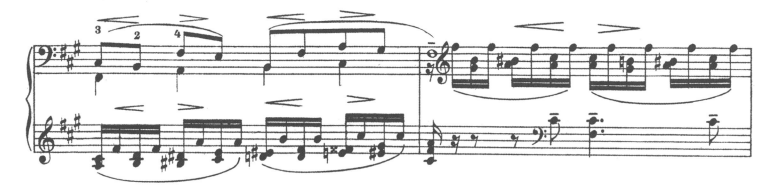

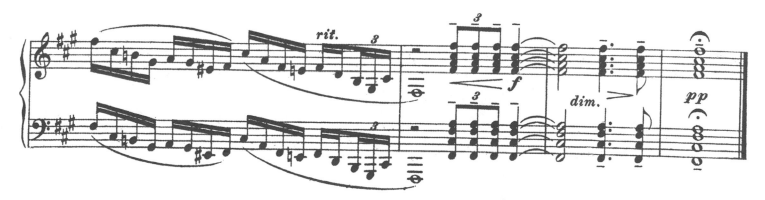

Prelude
in D Major

Sergei Rachmaninoff
Op. 23, No. 4

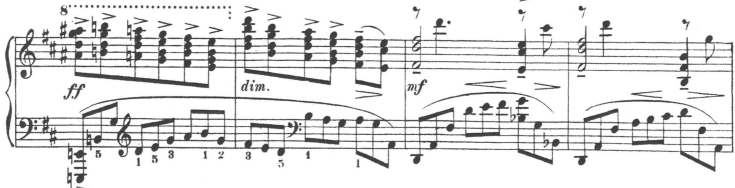

Prelude
in G minor

Sergei Rachmaninoff
Op. 23, No. 5

Alla marcia (♩=108)

Un poco meno mosso

poco a poco accelerando e cresc. al Tempo I

Tempo I

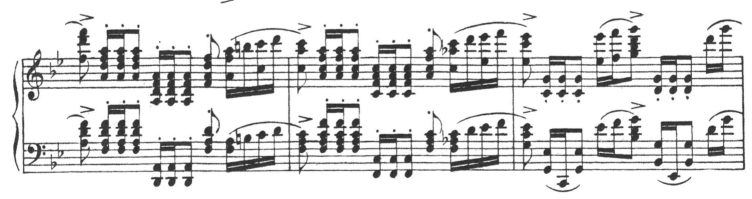

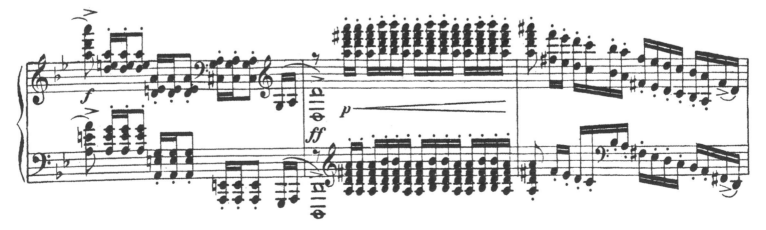

Prelude
in G-flat Major

Sergei Rachmaninoff
Op. 23, No. 10

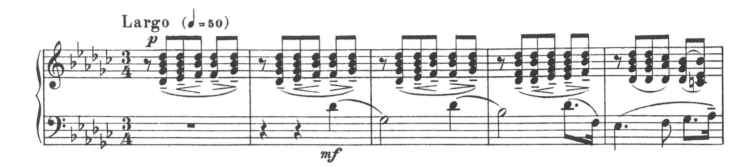

Prelude
in G Major

Sergei Rachmaninoff
Op. 32, No. 5

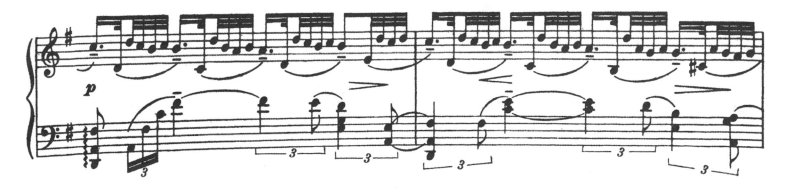

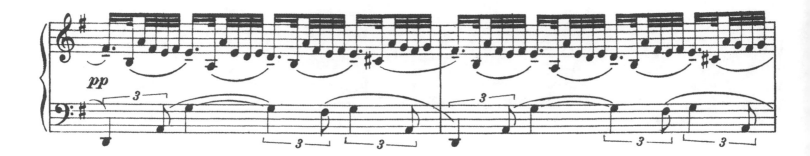

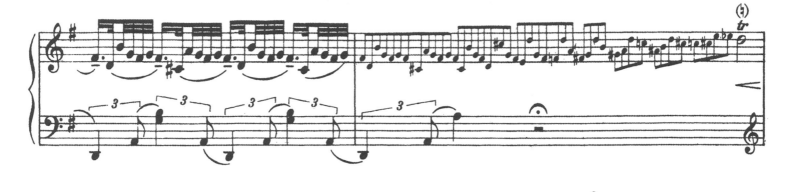

Prelude
in B minor

Sergei Rachmaninoff
Op. 32, No. 10

L'istesso tempo

Prelude
in G-sharp minor

Sergei Rachmaninoff
Op. 32, No. 12

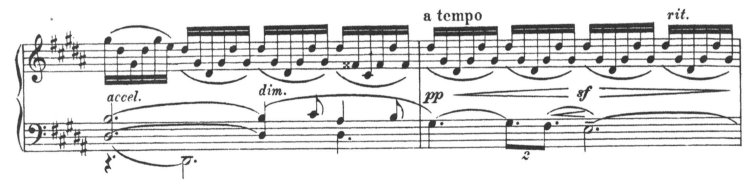

à Mademoiselle Jeanne Leleu

Prélude

Maurice Ravel

Lento assai e molto espressivo (free in rhythm) ♩ = 60

Ritenuto   **A tempo**

Ritenuto

Molto lento

Prelude
in A minor

Alexander Scriabin
Op. 11, No. 2

Allegretto ♩ = 138

accel.　　　　　　　　　　　rit.

Prelude
in E minor

Alexander Scriabin
Op. 11, No. 4

Prelude
in D Major

Alexander Scriabin
Op. 11, No. 5

Prelude
in G-flat Major

Alexander Scriabin
Op. 11, No. 13

Prelude
in G minor

Alexander Scriabin
Op. 11, No. 22

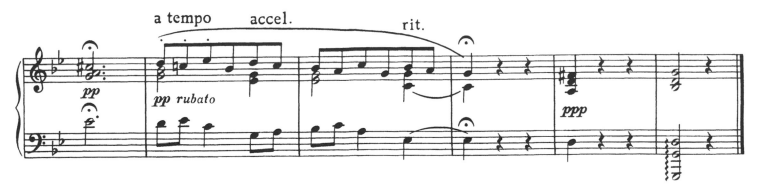

1) Scriabin often played the last chord in this measure *f*, followed by an immediate *pp* in the following bar, yielding an echo effect.

Prelude
in G Major

Alexander Scriabin
Op. 13, No. 3

Prelude
in E Major

Alexander Scriabin
Op. 15, No. 4

Andantino ♩ = 58 – 60

Prelude
in G-sharp minor

Alexander Scriabin
Op. 22, No. 1

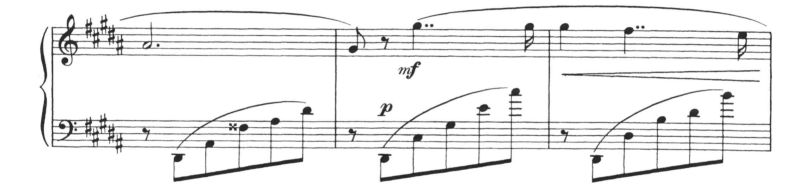

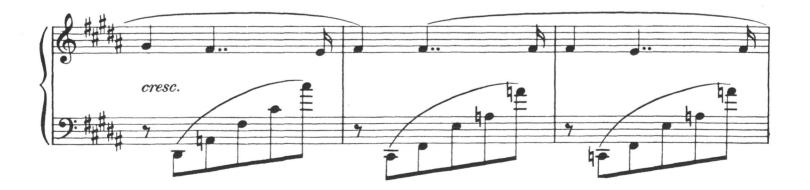

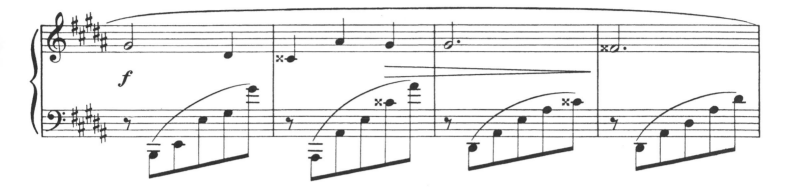

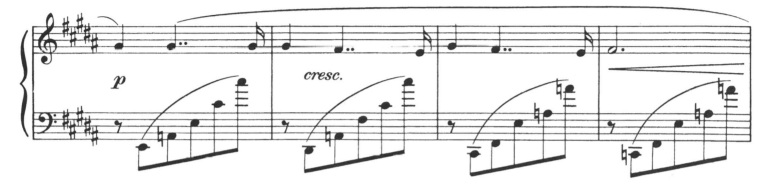

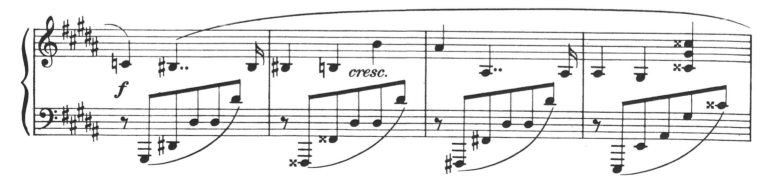

Prelude
in C-sharp minor

Alexander Scriabin
Op. 22, No. 2

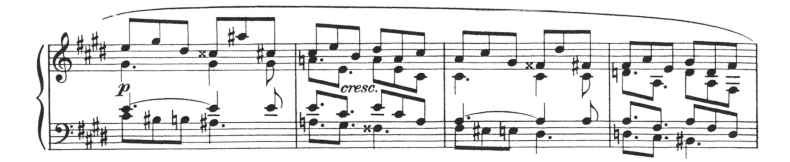

Prelude
in B Major

Alexander Scriabin
Op. 22, No. 3

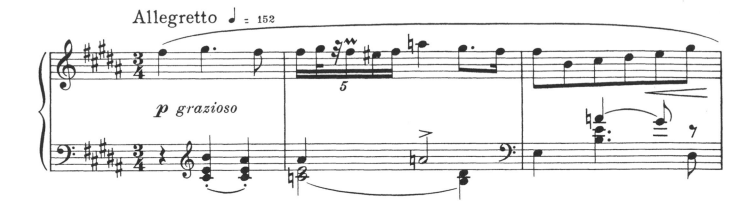

Prelude
in B minor

Alexander Scriabin
Op. 22, No. 4

Prelude
in B Major

Alexander Scriabin
Op. 27, No. 2

Prelude

Alexander Scriabin
Op. 74, No. 4

Lent, vague, indécis